conte

British & North American Readers:
Please note that Australian cup and
spoon measurements are metric. A quick
conversion guide appears on page 63.
A glossary explaining unfamiliar terms
and ingredients begins on page 60.

2 the gen on chocolate

Chocolate comes in varying qualities, from oversweet, cheap-tasting Easter egg chocolate, to superb, rich chocolate that has been conched (kneaded) for 100 hours to a smooth, creamy texture. The better the chocolate you use in your recipes, the better the result.

Cooking with chocolate

The best chocolate to cook with is the finest eating chocolate. Melt chocolate slowly in a double boiler or bowl over a pan of simmering water. It can also be melted in the microwave at 50 per cent power, but remember that chocolate retains its shape when heated in the microwave and you only know it's melted when you stir it. Watch that no water gets into the chocolate or it will 'seize', i.e, form a clump and harden, and you'll have to throw it out and start again.

Types of chocolate

Bittersweet/plain/dark chocolate: good quality bittersweet chocolate contains a high percentage of cocoa — from about 35 to 71 per cent, and is lightly sweetened.

Milk chocolate: this contains milk powder or condensed milk and usually has a lower percentage of cocoa than bittersweet chocolate, but more sugar.

White chocolate: made from cocoa butter and milk, it contains no chocolate liquor, which is why it's white.

Compound chocolate: this is cheaper than other chocolates because some of the cocoa butter has been replaced with oil, which changes the taste and texture of the chocolate. It is the easiest chocolate to cook with —practically foolproof, and the best chocolate for beginners to use.

triple chocolate
slice

125g butter, chopped

90g dark chocolate, chopped

90g milk chocolate, chopped

1/2 cup (100g) firmly packed brown sugar

2 eggs, beaten lightly

1 cup (150g) plain flour

2/3 cup (130g) white Choc Bits

Grease deep 19cm square cake pan, line base and 2 sides with baking paper, extending paper 2cm above edge of pan.

Combine butter with dark and milk chocolate in medium saucepan, stir over low heat until butter and chocolate melt; cool 2 minutes.

Stir in remaining ingredients; mix well. Pour mixture into prepared pan. Bake in moderate oven about 30 minutes; cool in pan. Cut into slices and serve dusted with sifted icing sugar, if desired.

milk chocolate
bubble slice

125g butter, chopped

200g milk chocolate, chopped

6 x 25g Milk Way bars, chopped

2 cups (70g) Rice Bubbles

1/2 cup (45g) desiccated coconut

150g packet coconut macaroons, chopped

1/4 cup (60ml) sour cream

2/3 cup (100g) dark chocolate Melts, melted

Grease 23cm square slab cake pan, line base and 2 sides with baking paper, extending paper 2cm above edge of pan.
Combine butter, milk chocolate and half the Milk Way bars in medium heavy-based saucepan, stir over low heat until mixture is just melted. Remove from heat, stir in Rice Bubbles, coconut, macaroons and sour cream; mix well. Stir in remaining Milky Way bars. Press mixture firmly into prepared pan. Drizzle with chocolate Melts; refrigerate until set. Cut into squares, then triangles.

double choc
almond slice

250g white chocolate Melts, melted

2 tablespoons vegetable oil

1 cup (160g) almond kernels, toasted

250g dark chocolate, chopped

2/3 cup (160ml) sweetened condensed milk

30g butter

1/4 teaspoon orange essence

Spread combined chocolate Melts and oil over base of oiled 19cm x 29cm rectangular slice pan, sprinkle with nuts; refrigerate until set. **Combine** dark chocolate, condensed milk and butter in medium heavy-based saucepan, stir over low heat until smooth, add essence. Spread mixture quickly over base; refrigerate until set. Cut into squares then triangles.

sicilian
cheesecake

125g plain chocolate biscuits, crushed finely

90g butter, melted

2 teaspoons gelatine

1 tablespoon water

500g ricotta cheese

²/₃ cup (110g) icing sugar mixture

2 teaspoons vanilla essence

60g finely grated dark chocolate

Serves 4

Line base and sides of 8cm x 26cm bar cake pan with baking paper.

Combine crumbs and butter in medium bowl; press firmly over base of prepared pan, refrigerate until firm.

Sprinkle gelatine over water in cup, stand in small saucepan of simmering water, stir until dissolved, cool slightly.

Beat cheese, icing sugar and essence in small bowl with electric mixer until smooth; fold in chocolate and gelatine mixture. Spoon mixture over base in pan, cover; refrigerate until firm.

icy chocolate pecan
truffles

¹/₄ cup (55g) caster sugar

2 egg yolks

¹/₃ cup (80ml) cream

125g dark chocolate, chopped roughly

1 tablespoon Grand Marnier

¹/₂ cup (60g) pecans, toasted, chopped finely

Whisk sugar and egg yolks in small heatproof bowl until thick. Bring cream to boil in small saucepan, gradually whisk hot cream into egg yolk mixture. Place bowl over saucepan of simmering water, stir over heat about 5 minutes or until mixture thickens slightly. Remove from heat, add chocolate, stir until melted. Stir in liqueur, cover; freeze until mixture is firm. Roll rounded teaspoons of mixture into balls, roll in nuts; freeze. Serve frozen.

Makes about 40

10 fruit and nut
choc chip cookies

125g butter, chopped

$1/2$ cup (100g) firmly packed brown sugar

1 egg, beaten lightly

$1^1/2$ cups (225g) self-raising flour

$1/4$ cup (20g) rolled oats

$1/2$ cup (80g) chopped seeded dates

$1/2$ cup (60g) chopped pecans, toasted

$1/2$ cup (95g) dark Choc Bits

Beat butter, sugar and egg in small bowl with electric mixer until smooth. Stir in remaining ingredients; mix well. Roll level tablespoons of mixture into balls, place about 5cm apart on greased oven trays, flatten slightly with a floured fork. Bake in moderate oven about 15 minutes or until browned. Stand 5 minutes before lifting onto wire rack to cool.

Makes about 30

chocolate toffee triangles

185g butter, softened

³/₄ cup (150g) firmly packed brown sugar

1 egg, beaten lightly

2 cups (300g) plain flour

²/₃ cup (130g) milk Choc Bits

³/₄ cup (110g) chopped raw peanuts

Grease 20cm x 30cm lamington pan, line base and 2 long sides with baking paper, extending paper 2cm above edge of pan.
Beat butter, sugar and egg in a medium bowl with electric mixer until changed to a lighter colour. Stir in flour and Choc Bits. Press over base of prepared pan, sprinkle with nuts, pressing down firmly; bake in moderate oven about 45 minutes. Cool in pan, before cutting into triangles. Dust with sifted icing sugar, if desired.

12

triple treat
chocolate muffins

90g butter, melted

2¹/₂ cups (375g) self-raising flour

¹/₂ cup (50g) cocoa powder, sifted

³/₄ cup (165g) caster sugar

1 egg, beaten lightly

1¹/₃ cups (330ml) milk

³/₄ cup (135g) chopped white chocolate

¹/₂ cup (90g) chopped milk chocolate

Grease 12-hole (¹/₃-cup/80ml-capacity) muffin pan. **Combine** all ingredients in large bowl, stir until just combined. Spoon mixture into prepared pan. Bake in moderately hot oven about 25 minutes. Turn onto wire rack to cool.

Makes 12

14 chocolate
fudge sauce

1/2 cup (125ml) cream

1/4 cup (55g) caster sugar

2 teaspoons cornflour

2 teaspoons water

125g dark chocolate, chopped

2 tablespoons brandy

Combine cream and sugar in medium saucepan, stir over heat, without boiling, until sugar is dissolved. Stir in blended cornflour and water, stir over heat until sauce boils and thickens. Remove from heat, add chocolate and brandy, stir until smooth.
Serve hot, warm or cold over ice-cream.

Makes about 1¾ cups (430ml)

mississippi

mud cake

250g cold unsalted butter, chopped

150g dark chocolate, chopped

2 cups (440g) caster sugar

1 cup (250ml) water

1/3 cup (80ml) whisky

1 tablespoon dry instant coffee

1 1/2 cups (225g) plain flour

1/4 cup (35g) self-raising flour

1/4 cup (25g) cocoa powder

2 eggs, beaten lightly

Grease 23cm square slab cake pan, line base with baking paper. **Combine** butter, chocolate, sugar, water, whisky and coffee in medium saucepan, stir over heat until butter and chocolate melt. Transfer mixture to large bowl; cool. Stir in sifted flours and cocoa, then eggs; pour mixture into prepared pan. **Bake** in moderately slow oven 1 1/4 hours. Stand cake in pan 30 minutes; turn onto wire rack to cool. Serve dusted with sifted icing sugar, if desired.

16 choc brownie
muffins

2 cups (300g) self-raising flour

1/3 cup (35g) cocoa powder

1/3 cup (75g) caster sugar

60g butter, melted

1/2 cup (95g) dark Choc Bits

1/2 cup (75g) shelled pistachios, chopped

1/2 cup (125ml) Nutella

1 egg, beaten lightly

3/4 cup (180ml) milk

1/2 cup (125ml) sour cream

Grease 12-hole (1/3-cup/80ml-capacity) muffin pan.
Sift dry ingredients into large bowl, stir in remaining ingredients. Spoon mixture into prepared pan. Bake in moderately hot oven about 20 minutes. Turn onto wire rack to cool.

Makes 12

caramel

chocolate brownies

185g unsalted butter, chopped

200g dark chocolate, chopped

1$\frac{1}{2}$ cups (330g) caster sugar

3 eggs, beaten lightly

1$\frac{2}{3}$ cups (250g) plain flour

$\frac{1}{3}$ cup (35g) cocoa powder

200g packet Jersey caramels, sliced

Grease 23cm square slab cake pan, line base with baking paper.
Combine butter and chocolate in medium saucepan, stir over heat until chocolate melts. Transfer mixture to large bowl, stir in sugar and eggs. Stir in sifted flour and cocoa until just combined.
Spread half the mixture over base of prepared pan, top with caramels, then remaining mixture. Bake in moderate oven about 40 minutes. Cool in pan. Cut into squares. Dust with extra sifted cocoa if desired and decorate with white chocolate curls.

the ultimate

chocolate sundae

2 litres (8 cups) chocolate ice-cream, softened

60g Mars Bar, chopped

1/4 cup (45g) milk Choc Bits

1/4 cup (45g) white Choc Bits

chocolate fudge sauce

1/2 cup (125ml) cream

2 tablespoons caster sugar

2 teaspoons cornflour

2 teaspoons water

2 x 60g Mars Bars, chopped finely

50g dark chocolate, chopped finely

Combine half the ice-cream with Mars Bar in large bowl. Spoon ice-cream into 14cm x 21cm loaf pan, cover with foil; freeze until firm.

Combine remaining ice-cream with both Choc Bits in large bowl. Spoon ice-cream into 14cm x 21cm loaf pan, cover with foil; freeze until firm.

Layer small scoops of each ice-cream into serving dishes; top with warm Chocolate Fudge Sauce.

Chocolate Fudge Sauce Combine cream and sugar in medium saucepan, stir over heat, without boiling, until sugar is dissolved. Stir in blended cornflour and water, stir over heat until sauce boils and thickens. Remove from heat; add Mars Bars and chocolate, stir until smooth.

Serves 6 to 8

20 bubble
truffles

2/3 cup (160ml) cream

300g dark chocolate, chopped

2 teaspoons dark rum

2 cups (70g) Rice Bubbles

50g dark chocolate Melts, melted

Bring cream to boil in medium saucepan, remove from heat. Stir in dark chocolate and rum, stir until smooth; cover; refrigerate until firm. **Drop** level teaspoons of mixture into Rice Bubbles in bowl, roll into balls, coating truffle mixture in Rice Bubbles. Place truffles in paper confectionery cases; drizzle with chocolate Melts, refrigerate until firm.

Makes about 60

frozen
hazelnut mousse

¹/₃ cup (80ml) Nutella

2 eggs, separated

¹/₃ cup (75g) caster sugar

1 tablespoon water

300ml thickened cream

2 tablespoons chopped roasted hazelnuts

Wrap a piece of foil to extend 2cm above top edge of 4 x ¹/₂-cup (125ml) straight-sided dishes, secure with kitchen string.

Beat Nutella, egg yolks, sugar and water in small bowl with electric mixer until light and creamy. Transfer mixture to large bowl. Beat cream in small bowl with electric mixer until soft peaks form, fold into Nutella mixture. Beat egg whites in clean small bowl with electric mixer until soft peaks form, fold into Nutella mixture. Spoon mixture into prepared dishes, freeze until firm.

Remove foil from dishes, roll edges in nuts. Serve topped with whipped cream, if desired.

Makes 4

22 chunky choc-chip
drop cakes

125g butter

1/4 cup (50g) firmly packed brown sugar

1/4 cup (55g) caster sugar

1/4 cup (35g) self-raising flour

1/4 cup (35g) plain flour

1/2 cup (45g) desiccated coconut

3 cups (90g) Corn Flakes

1/2 cup (70g) crushed nuts

1/2 cup (95g) dark Choc Bits

1 egg, beaten lightly

Combine butter and sugars in small saucepan; stir over low heat until butter melts, cool.

Combine flours, coconut, Corn Flakes, nuts and Choc Bits in large bowl; stir in butter mixture and egg. Drop level tablespoons of mixture about 5cm apart onto greased oven trays. Bake in moderate oven about 12 minutes or until browned lightly. Stand cakes 5 minutes; loosen and cool on trays.

Makes about 35

chocolate
oat slice

90g butter

2 tablespoons golden syrup

$^1/_2$ cup (75g) milk chocolate Melts

2 cups (180g) rolled oats, toasted

$^1/_2$ cup (75g) shelled pistachios, toasted, chopped

$^1/_2$ cup (95g) dark Choc Bits

$^1/_4$ cup (20g) desiccated coconut

Grease 20cm round sandwich cake pan, line base with baking paper. **Combine** butter, golden syrup and chocolate Melts in small saucepan; stir over low heat until butter and chocolate melt. Combine oats, nuts, Choc Bits and coconut in large bowl; stir in butter mixture. Spread over base of prepared pan; cover, refrigerate until firm

¹/₃ cup (75g) caster sugar

1¹/₂ tablespoons cornflour

3 eggs, beaten lightly

1³/₄ cups (430ml) milk

120g milk chocolate, chopped

20g butter

Combine sugar, cornflour, eggs and milk in medium saucepan, stir over heat until mixture boils and thickens. Remove from heat, add chocolate and butter, stir until chocolate melts.

Pour mixture into 4 serving glasses, cover surface with greaseproof paper to prevent skin from forming. Refrigerate until set.

Makes 4

caramel chocolate cream
slice

250g packet Jersey caramels, chopped

100g white chocolate, chopped

$1/4$ cup (60ml) cream

1 tablespoon light corn syrup

200g packet Tim Tams, chopped

100g white chocolate Melts, melted

Grease 23cm square slab cake pan, line base and 2 sides with baking paper, extending paper 2cm above edge of pan.

Combine caramels, chopped chocolate, cream and corn syrup in medium heatproof bowl, stir over pan of simmering water until smooth; gently stir in Tim Tams. Spread mixture into prepared pan; refrigerate until set. Cut into triangles; drizzle with chocolate Melts.

chocolate
cherry crumbles

2 x 425g cans seeded black cherries in syrup

2 teaspoons finely grated orange rind

1/4 cup (60ml) orange juice

3 teaspoons cornflour

1 tablespoon water

crumble topping

2/3 cup (100g) plain flour

1 1/2 tablespoons cocoa powder

90g butter, chopped

1/3 cup (75g) firmly packed brown sugar

1/3 cup (30g) desiccated coconut

Combine undrained cherries, half the rind, juice and blended cornflour and water in medium saucepan, stir over heat until mixture boils and thickens. Spoon cherry mixture into 4 x 1-cup (250ml) heatproof dishes. Sprinkle with Crumble Topping. Bake in moderate oven about 20 minutes or until topping is browned lightly.
Crumble Topping Sift flour and cocoa into small bowl, rub in butter. Add sugar, coconut and remaining rind; mix well.

Makes 4

brownie cake

185g butter, melted

1¹/₂ cups (330g) caster sugar

3 eggs

²/₃ cup (100g) plain flour

¹/₂ cup (50g) cocoa powder

50g after-dinner mints, chopped roughly.

Grease deep 22cm round cake pan, line base and side with baking paper.

Place butter and sugar in medium bowl, whisk until combined. Whisk in eggs, 1 at a time, whisking well after each addition. Stir in sifted flour and cocoa. Spread mixture into prepared pan.

Push pieces of mints into mixture so that mints are covered by cake mixture and do not touch side of pan. Bake in moderate oven about 1 hour or until just firm. Stand cake in pan 5 minutes; turn onto wire rack to cool.

Serve dusted with sifted icing sugar and cocoa powder, if desired.

rum ball
bar

100g dark chocolate, chopped

30g butter

4¹/₂ cups (450g) plain cake crumbs

¹/₃ cup (35g) cocoa powder

¹/₄ cup (40g) chopped raisins

¹/₄ cup (60ml) raspberry jam

2 tablespoons dark rum

2 tablespoons water

Grease 8cm x 26cm bar cake pan, line base and 2 long sides with baking paper, extending paper 2cm above edge of pan.

Melt combined chocolate and butter in small bowl over saucepan of simmering water, spread over base of pan; refrigerate until set.

Meanwhile, combine cake crumbs, sifted cocoa and raisins in large bowl. Warm then sieve jam; stir into mixture with rum and water. Spread over chocolate; cover, refrigerate until firm.

30 quick chocolate
mousse

125g dark chocolate, chopped

100g packet white marshmallows, chopped

300ml thickened cream

1 teaspoon vanilla essence

Combine chocolate and marshmallows in medium heatproof bowl, stir over saucepan of simmering water until melted. Remove from heat, gradually stir in cream and essence. Pour mixture into 4 x 1-cup (250ml) serving glasses. Refrigerate until set.

Makes 4

chocolate
turnovers

¹/₄ cup (60ml) Nutella

¹/₃ cup (65g) dark Choc Bits

¹/₄ cup (25g) hazelnut meal

1 sheet ready-rolled puff pastry

1 egg, beaten lightly

Combine Nutella, Choc Bits and nuts in small bowl. Cut pastry into quarters. Divide chocolate mixture among pastry. Brush edges of pastry with egg, fold in half diagonally to form triangles and enclose filling; press edges together with fork to seal. Place on greased oven tray; brush lightly with egg. Bake in hot oven about 15 minutes or until browned lightly.

Makes 4

chocolate treats

Dipping fruit, cookies, confectionery, even mini breadsticks in chocolate, instantly turns them into treats.

chocolate-dipped strawberries

100g dark chocolate, chopped

100g white chocolate, chopped

250g strawberries

Melt the chocolates in separate bowls over saucepans of simmering water.

Holding them by their green hulls, dip each berry into white chocolate to about $2/3$ of the way up the sides. Allow it to set. Then dip into dark chocolate to about $1/2$ way up the sides so there's a band of white chocolate between the dark chocolate and strawberry.

Makes 16

chocolate praline sticks

1/4 cup (55g) caster sugar

1 tablespoon water

2 tablespoons slivered almonds, toasted

35 mini grissini sticks (breadsticks)

100g dark chocolate, melted

Combine sugar and water in small saucepan, stir over heat, without boiling, until sugar dissolves; bring to boil, boil uncovered without stirring, until syrup is golden. Add almonds, pour onto lightly greased oven tray; cool.

When toffee is set, break into pieces, process until fine.
Dip each grissini stick into chocolate and then praline. Place on a tray lined with baking paper to set. Serve with coffee.
Makes 35

choc-dipped marshmallows

200g milk chocolate, chopped

100g white marshmallows

1 cup shredded toasted coconut

Melt chocolate in a small bowl over a pan of simmering water. Remove from heat.
Using a spoon and fork, dip each marshmallow into the chocolate, turning to coat evenly. Place marshmallows onto the coconut and roll to coat. Leave for a few minutes to set.
Makes 18

34 coconut

brownies

80g butter

100g dark chocolate, chopped

1¹/₂ cups (300g) firmly packed brown sugar

³/₄ cup (180ml) water

¹/₂ cup (75g) plain flour

¹/₄ cup (25g) cocoa powder

¹/₂ cup (45g) desiccated coconut

2 eggs, beaten lightly

Grease 23cm square slab cake pan, line base and sides with baking paper.

Combine butter, chocolate, sugar and water in medium saucepan; stir over low heat until butter and chocolate melt. Sift flour and cocoa into large bowl, add coconut, whisk in eggs and chocolate mixture. Pour mixture into prepared pan; bake in moderately slow oven for about 1 hour or until firm to touch. Cool brownies in pan before cutting into squares; dust with sifted icing sugar, if desired.

triple chocolate treat
ice-cream

2 litres (8 cups) chocolate ice-cream, softened

100g packet pink or white marshmallows, chopped

60g dark chocolate, melted

60g milk chocolate, melted

60g white chocolate, melted

Combine ice-cream and marshmallows in large bowl. Drizzle dark chocolate over ice-cream; mix well. Repeat with milk chocolate, then white chocolate. Spoon mixture into 14cm x 21cm loaf pan, cover with foil; freeze until firm.

Serves 6

36 chocolate refrigerator cake

1 teaspoon dry instant coffee

1¹/₂ tablespoons hot water

125g dark chocolate, melted

125g unsalted butter

¹/₃ cup (75g) caster sugar

2 teaspoons cocoa powder

2 eggs, separated

¹/₃ cup (70g) glace cherries, halved

¹/₃ cup (40g) chopped walnuts

150g packet coconut macaroons, chopped roughly

Grease 22cm springform tin, line base and side with baking paper.

Combine coffee and water in medium bowl, stir in chocolate, mix until smooth.

Beat butter and sugar in small bowl with electric mixer until light and fluffy, add cooked chocolate mixture, sifted cocoa and egg yolks; beat until smooth. Beat egg whites in clean small bowl with electric mixer until soft peaks form, gently fold into chocolate mixture. Fold in cherries and nuts.

Sprinkle macaroons over base of tin, pour over chocolate mixture; tap on bench to allow chocolate mixture to settle around macaroons. Cover, refrigerate until set. Sprinkle with chopped chocolate, if desired.

Serves 6 to 8

ice-cream

1 tablespoon dry
instant coffee

2 tablespoons boiling
water

2 tablespoons golden
syrup

1 litre (4 cups) vanilla
ice-cream, softened

¹/₂ cup (95g) dark
Choc Bits

Combine coffee, water and golden syrup in
small saucepan, stir over heat until coffee is
dissolved; cool. Stir coffee mixture into ice-
cream in large bowl, add Choc Bits; mix well.
Pour mixture into 14cm x 21cm loaf pan, cover
with foil; freeze until firm.

Serves 4

chocolate date
dessert cake

1 cup (160g) chopped seeded dates

250g butter, chopped

1³/₄ cups (430ml) water

1 cup (220g) caster sugar

¹/₃ cup (35g) cocoa powder

1²/₃ cups (250g) plain flour

1 teaspoon bicarbonate of soda

Grease 19cm x 29cm rectangular slice pan, line base with baking paper.
Combine dates, butter, water, sugar and sifted cocoa in medium saucepan. Bring to boil; simmer, uncovered, stirring, 5 minutes, cover, cool to room temperature.
Stir sifted flour and soda into mixture, pour into prepared pan. Bake in moderate oven about 40 minutes. Stand cake in pan 5 minutes; turn onto wire rack to cool.

40 white chocolate passionfruit
mousse

You will need about 6 passionfruit for this recipe.

250g packet cream cheese, chopped

1 cup (250ml) thickened cream

3/4 cup (120g) icing sugar mixture

250g white chocolate Melts, melted

1/2 cup (125ml) passionfruit pulp

2 tablespoons lemon juice

Beat cream cheese, cream, sugar and chocolate Melts in small bowl with electric mixer until smooth and thickened slightly. Fold in combined passionfruit and juice. Spoon mixture into 4 x 1-cup (250ml-capacity) glasses. Cover, refrigerate overnight.

Makes 4

chocolate date
torte

3 egg whites

1/2 cup caster sugar

1 cup slivered almonds, chopped finely

3/4 cup finely chopped dates

125g dark chocolate, grated

Grease 20cm springform tin, cover base with foil, grease foil. Beat egg whites in small bowl with electric mixer until soft peaks form. Gradually add sugar, beat until dissolved between each addition. Fold in almonds, dates and chocolate.

Spread mixture into prepared tin, baked in moderately slow oven for about 50 minutes or until firm; cool in oven with door ajar.

white chocolate, raspberry

and macadamia
blondies

125g butter, chopped

200g white chocolate, chopped

³/₄ cup (165g) caster sugar

2 eggs, beaten lightly

³/₄ cup (110g) plain flour

¹/₂ cup (75g) self-raising flour

100g white chocolate, chopped, extra

¹/₂ cup (75g) macadamias, toasted, chopped coarsely

150g fresh or frozen raspberries

Grease 23cm square slab cake pan, line base with baking paper.

Combine butter and chocolate in medium saucepan, stir over low heat until chocolate melts. Transfer mixture to large bowl; stir in remaining ingredients.

Spread mixture into prepared pan. Bake in moderate oven about 50 minutes or until firm. Cool in pan.

Cut into 9 squares, halve each diagonally to form 18 triangles. Dust blondies with sifted icing sugar, if desired.

Makes 18

chocolate custard

tartlets

4 x 7cm frozen sweet shortcrust tart cases

chocolate custard

1 cup (250ml) milk

1 tablespoon caster sugar

100g dark chocolate, chopped

1½ tablespoons custard powder

1 tablespoon milk, extra

1 tablespoon cream

Place cases on oven tray; bake in moderate oven about 15 minutes or until browned lightly; cool. Fill cases with Chocolate Custard.

Chocolate Custard Combine milk and sugar in small saucepan; bring to boil. Remove from heat, add chocolate, stir until melted. Stir in blended custard powder and extra milk; stir over heat until custard boils and thickens, cover, cool to room temperature. Beat custard and cream in small bowl with electric mixer until smooth and creamy.

Makes 4

rich chocolate and
croissant pudding

3 croissants

1/3 cup (80ml) Nutella

2 cups (500ml) milk

100g dark chocolate, chopped

2 tablespoons caster sugar

3 eggs, beaten lightly

Cut each croissant into 4 slices on the diagonal. Spread one side of croissant slices with Nutella.

Overlap slices in 1.5-litre (6-cup) shallow ovenproof dish.

Combine milk, chocolate and sugar in medium saucepan, stir over low heat until chocolate melts. Whisk milk mixture into eggs in medium bowl.

Gently pour milk mixture over croissant slices in dish, place in baking dish, with

enough boiling water to come halfway up side of ovenproof dish. Bake in moderately slow oven about 50 minutes or until just set in centre. **Serve** dusted with sifted icing sugar, if desired.

Serves 4 to 6

46 cherry ice-cream

bombe

1 litre (4 cups)
chocolate ice-cream

2 litres (8 cups) vanilla
ice-cream

$^1/_2$ cup (125g)
chopped red glace
cherries

$^1/_2$ cup (125g)
chopped green glace
cherries

$^1/_3$ cup (80ml)
chocolate-flavoured
ice-cream topping

Spoon chocolate ice-cream into 1.5-litre (6-cup capacity) pudding
steamer, press over base and side of steamer, leaving a hollow in centre.
Cover with foil, freeze until firm.

Beat vanilla ice-cream in large bowl with wooden spoon until just
softened, fold in both cherries.

Pour topping over chocolate ice-cream mixture in steamer, top with vanilla
ice-cream mixture, cover; freeze until firm.

Serves 6

baked chocolate
custard

3 eggs

¹/₄ cup (25g) cocoa powder

¹/₃ cup (75g) caster sugar

2 cups (500ml) milk

Whisk eggs, sifted cocoa and sugar in large bowl until combined. Heat milk in a small saucepan, gradually whisk into egg mixture. Pour into 4 x ³/₄-cup (180-ml) ovenproof dishes.
Stand dishes in baking dish with enough hot water to come halfway up sides of ovenproof dishes. Bake in moderate oven 25 minutes. Reduce heat to moderately slow, bake about 20 minutes or until just set. Dust with sifted icing sugar, if desired.

Serves 4

chocolate mousse pavlova

2 teaspoons gelatine

1 tablespoon water

300g packaged pavlova

100g dark chocolate, melted

2 eggs, separated

3/4 cup (180ml) thickened cream

1 tablespoon caster sugar

Sprinkle gelatine over water in cup, stand in small saucepan of simmering water, stir until dissolved, cool slightly.

Using a knife, mark a circle, 3cm from edge of the pavlova. Press the inside of the circle with the back of a spoon to make a 3cm-deep hollow.

Combine the cooled chocolate and egg yolks together in medium bowl, stir in gelatine mixture. Beat cream and sugar in small bowl with electric mixer until soft peaks form, fold into chocolate mixture. Beat egg whites in clean small bowl with electric mixer until soft peaks form, fold into chocolate mixture. Spoon mixture into cavity of pavlova; spread mousse evenly using a spatula. Refrigerate until set.

Serves 6 to 8

50 rich
fudge cake

**You need the ingredients
listed on the packet of
cake mix for this recipe.**

*370g packet rich chocolate
cake mix*

*150g dark chocolate,
melted*

¹/₂ cup (125ml) sour cream

¹/₂ cup (125ml) Nutella

*¹/₂ cup (40g) flaked
almonds, toasted*

Grease deep 22cm round cake pan, line
base with baking paper.
Beat cake mix with packet ingredients,
cooled chocolate and cream in medium
bowl with electric mixer on low speed until
combined. Beat on medium speed
2 minutes, or until mixture has changed to
a lighter colour. Pour cake mixture into
prepared pan; bake in moderate oven
about 1 hour. Stand cake in pan
10 minutes; turn onto wire rack to cool.
Level top of cake; spread with Nutella;
sprinkle with nuts.

crunchy
choc peanut slice

4 x 60g Snickers bars, chopped

50g butter

1 tablespoon dark corn syrup

150g milk chocolate, chopped

1/2 cup (75g) unsalted roasted peanuts, chopped

2 1/2 cups (175g) Crunchy Nut corn flakes

Grease 23cm square slab cake pan, line base and 2 sides with baking paper, extending paper 2cm above edge of pan.

Combine Snickers, butter, corn syrup and chocolate in large heatproof bowl, stir over saucepan of simmering water until smooth. Remove from heat, stir in nuts and corn flakes. Press mixture into prepared pan; refrigerate until set.

52 almond chocolate
crescents

4 large sponge finger
biscuits, crushed

100g dark chocolate,
grated coarsely

$1/4$ cup (30g) almond
meal

60g butter, melted

1 sheet ready-rolled
puff pastry

1 egg, beaten lightly

Combine crumbs, chocolate, almond meal and butter in small bowl. Cut
pastry into 4 squares. Spoon one quarter of chocolate mixture diagonally
onto each pastry square. Roll pastry from one corner to the opposite
corner, turn ends to form crescent shape. Repeat with remaining
chocolate mixture and pastry squares. Place crescents on oven tray,
brush with egg; bake in moderately hot oven about 20 minutes or until
browned lightly. Serve dusted with sifted icing sugar, if desired.

Makes 4

fluffy

chocolate cake

cooking oil spray

125g butter, chopped

1 cup (220g) caster sugar

2 eggs, beaten lightly

1$^1/_2$ cups (225g) self-raising flour

$^1/_3$ cup (35g) cocoa powder

$^1/_2$ teaspoon bicarbonate of soda

1 cup (250ml) water

Coat 21cm baba pan with cooking oil spray.
Combine remaining ingredients in medium bowl, beat with electric mixer on low speed until ingredients are combined. Then, beat on medium speed until mixture is smooth and changed in colour. Pour mixture into prepared pan. Bake in moderate oven about 50 minutes. Stand cake in pan 5 minutes; turn onto wire rack to cool.
Dust cake with equal quantities sifted icing sugar and cocoa, if desired.

no-bowl
five-cup slice

1 cup (160g) sultanas
1 cup (190g) dark Choc Bits
1 cup (150g) unsalted roasted peanuts
1 cup (90g) desiccated coconut
1 cup (250ml) sweetened condensed milk
50g dark chocolate, melted

Grease 20cm x 30cm lamington pan, line base and 2 long sides with baking paper, extending paper 2cm above edge of pan.
Sprinkle pan with sultanas, Choc Bits, nuts and coconut. Drizzle with condensed milk.
Bake, covered in moderately hot oven 20 minutes. Reduce heat to moderate, uncover; bake 15 minutes, cool in pan. Drizzle melted chocolate over slice; leave to set before cutting.

chocolate slice

3 eggs

1 teaspoon vanilla essence

1 cup (200g) firmly packed brown sugar

3/4 cup (110g) plain flour

1/4 cup (35g) self-raising flour

125g butter, melted

250g dark chocolate, melted

3/4 cup (195g) crunchy peanut butter

1 cup (150g) unsalted roasted peanuts, chopped

Grease 20cm x 30cm lamington pan, line base and 2 long sides with baking paper, extending paper 2cm above edge of pan.
Beat eggs, essence and sugar in medium bowl with electric mixer about 3 minutes or until thick and pale in colour. Stir in remaining ingredients. Spread mixture into prepared pan. Bake in moderately slow oven about 30 minutes or until firm; cool in pan.

125g butter, chopped

1 teaspoon vanilla essence

1¹/₄ cups (250g) firmly packed brown sugar

1 egg

1 cup (150g) plain flour

¹/₄ cup (35g) self-raising flour

1 teaspoon bicarbonate of soda

¹/₃ cup (35g) cocoa powder

³/₄ cup (90g) chopped pecans, toasted

¹/₂ cup (85g) chopped raisins

¹/₂ cup (95g) dark Choc Bits

¹/₂ cup (75g) dark chocolate Melts, halved

Beat butter, essence, sugar and egg in medium bowl with electric mixer until smooth. Stir in sifted dry ingredients, then remaining ingredients.
Drop slightly rounded tablespoons of mixture about 5cm apart onto greased oven trays.
Bake in moderate oven about 12 minutes or until firm; cool on trays.
Makes about 24

58 chocolate
cream rice

1 litre (4 cups) milk

1/2 cup (100g) firmly packed brown sugar

2/3 cup (130g) white short-grain rice

100g dark chocolate, chopped

300ml thickened cream

30g dark chocolate, grated

Combine milk and sugar in medium, heavy-based saucepan, stir over heat until sugar is dissolved. Bring to boil, stir in rice. Simmer, covered, about 50 minutes or until almost all the milk has been absorbed, stirring several times during cooking. Remove from heat, add chopped chocolate, stir until chocolate melts; cool to room temperature.
Beat cream in small bowl with electric mixer until soft peaks form, fold half the cream into rice mixture. Spoon mixture into 4 serving dishes; refrigerate 1 hour. Decorate with remaining cream and grated chocolate.
Serves 4

rum'n'raisin
slice

100g butter

1/2 cup (110g) caster sugar

1 egg, beaten lightly

1 tablespoon dark rum

2 tablespoons cocoa powder

250g packet plain sweet biscuits, crushed finely

1/4 cup (60g) chopped glace cherries

3/4 cup (120g) seeded chopped dates

1/2 cup (85g) raisins

1/2 cup (70g) slivered almonds, toasted

Grease 19cm x 29cm rectangular slice pan; cover base and 2 long sides with baking paper, extending paper 2cm above edge of pan.

Combine butter and sugar in small saucepan; stir over heat until sugar dissolves, remove from heat, stand 5 minutes. Stir in egg and rum. Sift cocoa into medium bowl, stir in biscuit crumbs, fruit, nuts and butter mixture. Press over base of prepared pan; cover, refrigerate until firm.

glossary

almonds
blanched: skins removed.
flaked: paper-thin slices.
ground: also known as
   almond meal.
slivered: small lengthways-
   cut pieces.
amaretti biscuits small
   Italian-style macaroons
   based on ground almonds.
bicarbonate of soda also
   known as baking soda.
biscuits
Choc Crunch: an uniced,
   plain, hard chocolate
   biscuit.
Milk Coffee: an uniced, plain
   biscuit sweetened with
   golden syrup.
Tim Tams: chocolate biscuits
   coated in chocolate; made
   from chocolate, flour, sugar,
   oil, golden syrup, milk
   powder and cocoa.
butter use salted or unsalted
   ("sweet") butter; 125g is
   equal to 1 stick butter.
cheese
cream: soft milk cheese
   commonly known as
   "Philadelphia" or "Philly".
mascarpone: a fresh, thick,
   triple-cream cheese with a
   delicately sweet, slightly
   sour taste.
ricotta: a sweet, fairly moist
   fresh curd cheese having a
   low fat content.
cherries, glace these are
   cooked in heavy sugar
   syrup and then dried.
chestnut puree an
   unsweetened puree of
   chestnuts. Do not confuse
   with the sweetened

flavoured chestnut spread.
chestnut puree, sweetened
   canned, sweetened
   chestnut puree with the
   addition of vanilla.
chestnut spread also known
   as creme de marrons, a
   French product made of
   pureed chestnuts, candied
   chestnut pieces, sugar,
   glucose syrup and vanilla.
   Available from good
   delicatessens.
chocolate
bittersweet: also known as
   dark chocolate or plain
   chocolate. It is good quality
   eating chocolate with a low
   sugar content. We use the
   Lindt brand.
choc bits: also known as
   chocolate chips and
   chocolate morsels;
   available in milk, white
   and dark chocolate.
   Made of cocoa liquor,
   cocoa butter, sugar and
   an emulsifier, these hold
   their shape in baking and
   are ideal for decorating.
dark: eating chocolate;
   made of cocoa liquor,
   cocoa butter and sugar.
drinking: sweetened cocoa
   powder.
melts: available in milk,
   white and dark chocolate.
   Made of sugar, vegetable
   fats, milk solids, cocoa
   powder, butter oil and
   emulsifiers, these are good
   for melting and moulding.
white: eating chocolate.
chocolate rollettes 9cm long
   chocolate sponge rolls filled

with cream; purchased in
   250g packets of 6.
coconut, desiccated
   unsweetened,
   concentrated, dried
   shredded coconut.
coconut macaroons made
   from coconut, egg white
   and cornflour.
cornflour also known as
   cornstarch; used as a
   thickening agent in
   cooking.
corn syrup an imported
   product. It is available in
   light or dark colour; either
   can be substituted for the
   other; glucose syrup (liquid
   glucose) can be
   substituted.
cream
fresh (minimum fat content
   35%): also known as pure
   cream and pouring cream;
   has no additives like
   commercially thickened
   cream.
sour (minimum fat content
   35%): a thick,
   commercially-cultured
   soured cream good for
   dips, toppings and baked
   cheesecakes.
thickened (minimum fat
   content 35%): a whipping
   cream containing a
   thickener.
Crunchy Nut Corn Flakes
   crisp corn flakes encrusted
   with nuts and honey.
custard powder packaged,
   vanilla pudding mixture.
flour
white plain: an all-purpose
   flour, made from wheat.

white self-raising: plain flour sifted with baking powder in the proportion of 1 cup flour to 2 teaspoons baking powder.

gelatine (gelatin): we used powdered gelatine. It is also available in sheet form known as leaf gelatine.

golden syrup a byproduct of refined sugarcane; pure maple syrup or honey can be substituted.

Grand Marnier orange-flavoured liqueur based on cognac.

jam also known as preserve or conserve; most often made from fruit cooked in a sugar syrup until thick.

jersey caramels made from sugar, glucose, condensed milk, flour, oil and gelatine.

macadamia nuts native to Australia, rich and buttery nuts; store in refrigerator because of high oil content.

Mars bar a soft nougat and creamy caramel bar coated in milk chocolate.

milk we used full-cream homogenised milk unless otherwise specified.

sweetened condensed: a canned milk product consisting of milk with more than half the water content removed and sugar added to the milk which remains.

Milky Way bar made from chocolate, sugar, glucose, malt, water, butter and egg white.

Nutella chocolate hazelnut spread.

nuts to roast nuts, place them on a baking tray in a moderate oven, shaking the tray once or twice to ensure even roasting, until nuts are pale golden. Watch carefully; nuts burn easily. To remove skins, leave nuts to cool slightly, then rub off skins with a clean cloth.

peanut butter peanuts ground to a paste; available in crunchy and smooth varieties.

pistachio nuts pale green, delicately flavoured nuts inside hard off-white shells.

raisins dried sweet grapes.

Rice Bubbles rice crispies

rolled oats oat groats husked, steam-softened, flattened with rollers, dried and packaged for consumption as a cereal product.

rum liquor made from fermented sugarcane; available in dark or light varieties.

dark: we prefer to use an underproof rum (not overproof) for a more subtle flavour.

Snickers bar made from chocolate, peanuts, glucose, sugar, milk powder, butter and egg white.

sponge finger biscuits also known as Savoiardi, Savoy biscuits or ladyfingers. They are Italian-style, crisp biscuits made from a sponge-cake mixture.

sugar we used coarse, granulated table sugar, also known as crystal sugar, unless otherwise specified.

brown: an extremely soft, fine granulated sugar retaining molasses for its characteristic colour and flavour.

caster: also known as superfine or finely granulated table sugar.

icing mixture: also known as confectioners' sugar or powdered sugar; granulated sugar crushed together with a small amount (about 3%) cornflour added.

sultanas golden raisins.

Tia Maria coffee-flavoured liqueur.

vanilla bean dried bean of the vanilla orchid, if used whole it can be used repeatedly. Simply wash in warm water after use, dry well and store in airtight container.

facts and figures 63

These conversions are approximate only, but the difference between an exact and the approximate conversion of various liquid and dry measures is minimal and will not affect your cooking results.

Measuring equipment

The difference between one country's measuring cups and another's is, at most, within a 2 or 3 teaspoon variance. (For the record, 1 Australian metric measuring cup holds approximately 250ml.) The most accurate way of measuring dry ingredients is to weigh them. For liquids, use a clear glass or plastic jug having metric markings.

Note: NZ, Canada, USA and UK all use 15ml tablespoons. Australian tablespoons measure 20ml.
All cup and spoon measurements are level.

How to measure

When using graduated measuring cups, shake dry ingredients loosely into the appropriate cup. Do not tap the cup on a bench or tightly pack the ingredients unless directed to do so. Level the top of measuring cups and measuring spoons with a knife. When measuring liquids, place a clear glass or plastic jug having metric markings on a flat surface to check accuracy at eye level.

Dry Measures

metric	imperial
15g	1/2oz
30g	1oz
60g	2oz
90g	3oz
125g	4oz (1/4lb)
155g	5oz
185g	6oz
220g	7oz
250g	8oz (1/2lb)
280g	9oz
315g	10oz
345g	11oz
375g	12oz (3/4lb)
410g	13oz
440g	14oz
470g	15oz
500g	16oz (1lb)
750g	24oz (11/2lb)
1kg	32oz (2lb)

We use large eggs having an average weight of 60g.

Liquid Measures

metric	imperial
30ml	1 fluid oz
60ml	2 fluid oz
100ml	3 fluid oz
125ml	4 fluid oz
150ml	5 fluid oz (1/4 pint/1 gill)
190ml	6 fluid oz
250ml (1cup)	8 fluid oz
300ml	10 fluid oz (1/2 pint)
500ml	16 fluid oz
600ml	20 fluid oz (1 pint)
1000ml (1litre)	13/4 pints

Helpful Measures

metric	imperial
3mm	1/8in
6mm	1/4in
1cm	1/2in
2cm	3/4in
2.5cm	1in
6cm	21/2in
8cm	3in
20cm	8in
23cm	9in
25cm	10in
30cm	12in (1ft)

Oven Temperatures

These oven temperatures are only a guide.
Always check the manufacturer's manual.

	C°(Celsius)	F°(Fahrenheit)	Gas Mark
Very slow	120	250	1
Slow	150	300	2
Moderately slow	160	325	3
Moderate	180 –190	350 – 375	4
Moderately hot	200 – 210	400 – 425	5
Hot	220 – 230	450 – 475	6
Very hot	240 – 250	500 – 525	7

Food editor Pamela Clark
Associate food editor Karen Hammial
Assistant food editor Kathy McGarry
Assistant recipe editor Elizabeth Hooper

HOME LIBRARY STAFF
Editor-in-chief Mary Coleman
Marketing manager Nicole Pizanis
Editor Susan Tomnay
Concept design Jackie Richards
Designer Jackie Richards
Group publisher Tim Trumper
Chief executive officer John Alexander

Produced by *The Australian Women's Weekly*
Home Library, Sydney.

Colour separations by
ACP Colour Graphics Pty Ltd, Sydney.
Printing by Dai Nippon, Korea.

Published by ACP Publishing Pty Limited,
54 Park St, Sydney; GPO Box 4088, Sydney,
NSW 1028. Ph: (02) 9282 8618
Fax: (02) 9267 9438.

AWWHomeLib@publishing.acp.com.au

Australia Distributed by Network Distribution
Company, GPO Box 4088, Sydney, NSW 1028.
Ph: (02) 9282 8777 Fax: (02) 9264 3278.

United Kingdom Distributed by Australian
Consolidated Press (UK), Moulton Park
Business Centre, Red House Rd, Moulton Park,
Northampton, NN3 6AQ. Ph: (01604) 497 531
Fax: (01604) 497 533 Acpukltd@aol.com

Canada Distributed by Whitecap Books Ltd,
351 Lynn Ave, North Vancouver, BC, V7J 2C4,
Ph: (604) 980 9852.

New Zealand Distributed by Netlink Distribution
Company, 17B Hargreaves St, Level 5,
College Hill, Auckland 1, Ph: (9) 302 7616.

South Africa Distributed by PSD Promotions
(Pty) Ltd,PO Box 1175, Isando 1600, SA,
Ph: (011) 392 6065.
CNA Limited, Newsstand Division, PO Box
10799, Johannesburg 2000. Ph: (011) 491 7500.

Sweet and Simple: Chocolate

Includes index.
ISBN 1 86396 173 9.

1. Cookery (Chocolate) I Title: Australian
Women's Weekly. (Series: Australian Women's
Weekly sweet and simple mini series).
641.3374

© ACP Publishing Pty Limited 2000
ACN 053 273 546

Cover: Chocolate date torte, page 41.
Stylist: Jacqui Hing
Photographer Scott Cameron
Back cover: No-bowl five-cup slice, page 55

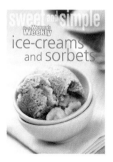

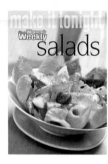